D0852595

INNOVATION
NATION

Tundra Books, an imprint of Penguin Random House Canada Young Readers,
a Penguin Random House Company

Library and Archives Canada Cataloguing in Publication is available upon request.

Published simultaneously in the United States of America by Tundra Books of Northern New York,
an imprint of Penguin Random House Canada Young Readers, a Penguin Random House Company

Library of Congress Control Number: 2017939202

Text adaptation by Mary Beth Leatherdale
Designed by Lisa Jager
Project managed by Elizabeth Kribs
The artwork in this book was rendered digitally. The text was set in Brandon Text.

All proceeds from *Innovation Nation* will be directed to the Rideau Hall Foundation for activities and
programs that inspire and support innovation by Canadians in every province and territory.

Printed and bound in Canada

www.penguinrandomhouse.ca

1 2 3 4 5   21 20 19 18 17

Penguin
Random House
tundra | TUNDRA BOOKS

INNOVATION NATION

HOW CANADIAN INNOVATORS MADE THE WORLD

SMARTER, SMALLER, KINDER, SAFER, HEALTHIER, WEALTHIER, AND HAPPIER

DAVID JOHNSTON & TOM JENKINS

ILLUSTRATED BY JOSH HOLINATY

ADAPTED BY MARY BETH LEATHERDALE

tundra

CONTENTS

WHAT MAKES CANADIANS SO INNOVATIVE?

Every human is creative. Every community is inventive. Yet some nations have populations that seem to be particularly good at approaching problems in ways that make creative thinking easier. Canada is one of those nations. We don't like to brag, but Canadian innovations are used across the country and around the world every day. Turn on a light bulb? Yup, that's a Canadian innovation. Zip up your jacket? Thank Canada. Enjoy an after-school PB&J? Yes, even peanut butter came from a rich Canadian idea.

As you read through *Innovation Nation*, you'll see the factors that have contributed to making Canada so innovative. The first is rooted deep in the history of the land. For thousands of years, First Nations and Inuit peoples explored and shared the land we now call Canada. To cope with the diverse geography and climate, they needed to be very ingenious. Many early Indigenous innovations such as duck decoys, canoes, and life jackets are still used today.

Canada's varied climate and vast geography continue to inspire innovation.

Our often-extreme weather led to the development of life-saving technologies such as the foghorn and the snowmobile. The desire to stay connected in our vast country sparked new communication technology like the telephone.

Another Canadian quality that's been good for innovation is our tendency to want to get along. Canadians are often teased for being polite, following the rules, and, sorry to say, over-apologizing. However, our belief that good relationships are critical to success has paid off. Canadian history has proven that when research teams collaborate they produce better results and can achieve extraordinary breakthroughs like telesurgery.

All of these things—plus timing—have served Canadian innovation well. In the 19th century, around the time of Confederation, new scientific techniques became popular. The new modern sciences required the "invention" of new instruments, machines, processes, and approaches. Given our innovative spirit, it's not surprising that many of them were created by Canadians.

We wrote this book to celebrate the history and spirit of creativity in Canada. On the pages that follow, you will learn about fifty Canadian innovations that have changed the world. There has never has been a better time to have an idea, share it, improve it, and turn it into something that changes something else for the better. So, future Canadian innovators, read on and good luck!

How Canadian Innovators Made the World

SMARTER

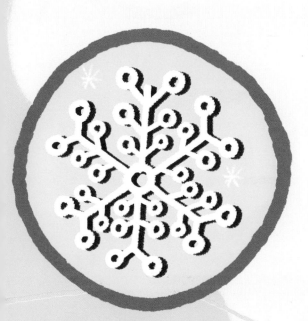

Whether it's the shining example of the electric light bulb or life-changing cell phone tech like the BlackBerry, Canadian innovators' bright ideas light up the world in ways that are smarter than anything that came before.

Duck Decoy

For thousands of years, the Cree and Ojibway people of the Great Lakes relied on their hunting skills to survive. Because their bow and arrows couldn't reach birds flying overhead, the hunters developed strategies to make sure the waterfowl and game birds came to them. To lure a tasty duck or a wild turkey, the First Nations hunters made bird decoys out of reeds, cattails, bulrushes, and other plants. Then, they placed the decoys in a marsh or pond where birds liked to roost and waited nearby. The wild birds flocked to the lifelike decoys. Once the birds were close, the First Nations hunters could use their nets, snares, arrows, and spears to capture them. European settlers who came to Canada started using the First Nations hunters' technique. Today, thousands of years later, this tradition continues to be passed down and hunters still use duck decoys to lure wild game birds.

If You Build It They Will Come

A Bright Idea

Light Bulb

In the 1800s, candles and gas lamps were used to light up the night. Unfortunately, they were dirty and dangerous, and often started fires—until a couple of creative Canadians came up with a bright idea.

Amateur scientists Henry Woodward and Matthew Evans liked to get together in the evening to do experiments. One night, the duo made an illuminating discovery. They noticed a spark of light when a metal wire touched their old-fashioned battery. Immediately, they realized that if they could contain the spark in a globe they could make a new kind of lamp—one that created artificial light using electricity. After many nights of testing, in 1874, their prototype light bulb was ready.

The pair patented their invention in Canada and the United States. They tried for years to find investors to fund the development of their light bulbs, with no luck. Finally, Woodward and Evans were forced to sell their patent to an American inventor. After refining their design, Thomas Edison unveiled the amazing new electric light bulb to the world. The American inventor became famous thanks to these bright Canadian innovators.

Electric Radio

In the early 1900s, radios were expensive and hard to use. They were powered by large batteries that took up a lot of space and leaked acid. Even more frustrating, the loud hum of the batteries made it hard to hear what was being broadcast.

A young inventor, Edward Rogers Sr., was determined to develop a better radio, one that would run on the electricity people already had in their homes. After a lot of experimentation and research, he did just that. In 1925, Rogers developed a tube that could use electricity to receive and amplify sound. With this innovation, his dream of an all-electric radio became a reality.

Rogers's electric radio was a hit in Canada and around the world. He didn't stop there, though. Rogers started a company that made radios. Plus, to make sure people had something worth listening to, he created CFRB—Canada's First Rogers Batteryless broadcasting station—a Toronto-based radio channel that you can still tune into now. Rogers's son, Ted, went on to start the Rogers cable TV, Internet, and cell phone companies that you may know today. But that's another story . . .

Dump Truck

Diggers and dumpers are the superstars of today's construction sites. But dump trucks were not always the big movers and shakers on the scene. Once upon a time, huge loads of dirt or gravel had to be shovelled out of a truck by hand. That is, until New Brunswicker Robert Mawhinney came up with a sweat-saving scheme.

In 1920, he designed a truck with a simple dump box in the back. Using materials he had on hand— a ship's mast, a cable, and a winch—he figured out how to lift the box and spill the dirt. By turning a simple crank on the winch, the cable would lift the front end of the box high enough to dump its load out the opened back.

Mawhinney's idea was a huge success. Now, dump trucks rule construction sites everywhere.

Take a Load Off

Aniuvak snow melted for water

Igluksattiavak snow that is good for building

Natiruviartuq drifting snow

Agilluqqaaq fresh snow in the springtime

Masak melting snow

Pukaq dry sandy snow

Qannirtuq snowing

Mauja soft, deep snow that is hard to walk on

Sitilluqqaq old snow, hardened by strong winds

Imingnaqtuq snow that crunches

Snow Science

As Canadians, we know snow. The perfect packing snow to build a snowman. The fluffy powder that's just right for whooshing down the hill on a toboggan. And that wet, slushy stuff that soaks through your boots. But snow is just snow, isn't it? Think again.

The Inuit have many Inuktut words to distinguish one type of snow from another. They travel over snow and ice and use snow for building. So understanding its physical and mechanical properties—its strength at different temperatures and thicknesses—is critical to surviving life in the Far North.

George Klein, an innovative mechanical engineer, learned from the Inuit and studied the tools they used to find good snow for building and to test ice. He paired the traditional knowledge with modern technology to develop scientific instruments and processes to measure the hardness, depth, and surface qualities of snow and ice. Respect for Klein's system snowballed, and in 1951 it became the International Classification for Snow. Today, engineers still use it to improve the design and safety of bridges and buildings to make sure road and communications systems can weather the weather.

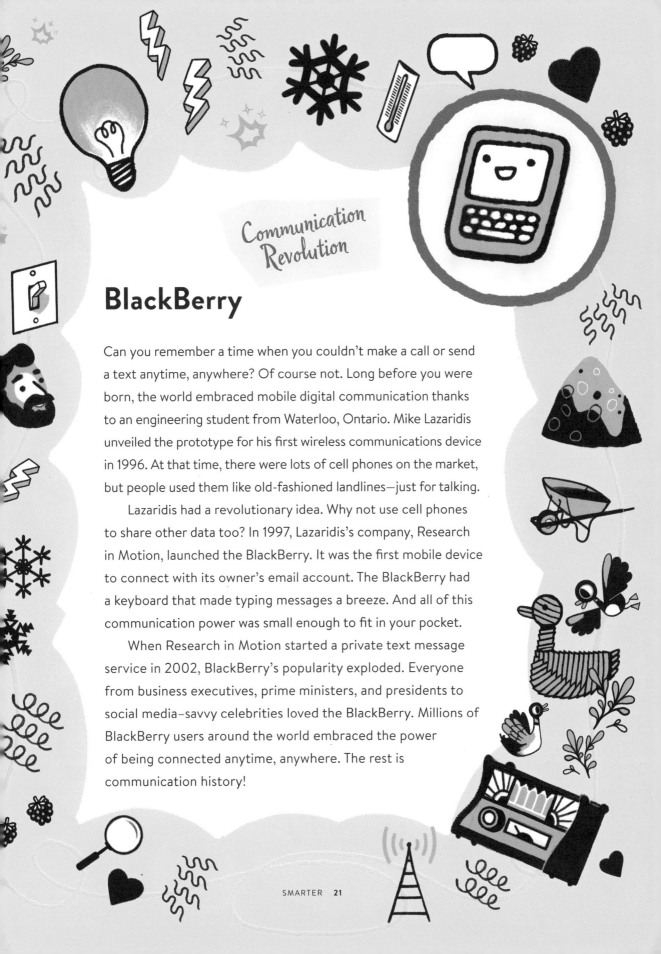

BlackBerry

Can you remember a time when you couldn't make a call or send a text anytime, anywhere? Of course not. Long before you were born, the world embraced mobile digital communication thanks to an engineering student from Waterloo, Ontario. Mike Lazaridis unveiled the prototype for his first wireless communications device in 1996. At that time, there were lots of cell phones on the market, but people used them like old-fashioned landlines—just for talking.

Lazaridis had a revolutionary idea. Why not use cell phones to share other data too? In 1997, Lazaridis's company, Research in Motion, launched the BlackBerry. It was the first mobile device to connect with its owner's email account. The BlackBerry had a keyboard that made typing messages a breeze. And all of this communication power was small enough to fit in your pocket.

When Research in Motion started a private text message service in 2002, BlackBerry's popularity exploded. Everyone from business executives, prime ministers, and presidents to social media–savvy celebrities loved the BlackBerry. Millions of BlackBerry users around the world embraced the power of being connected anytime, anywhere. The rest is communication history!

How Canadian
Innovators Made the World
SMALLER

When you live in the world's second-largest country, you have to work hard to close the distance between people. From transportation wonders like canoes and snowmobiles to pioneering communication devices like the telephone and walkie-talkies, Canadian innovations are making the country and the world smaller.

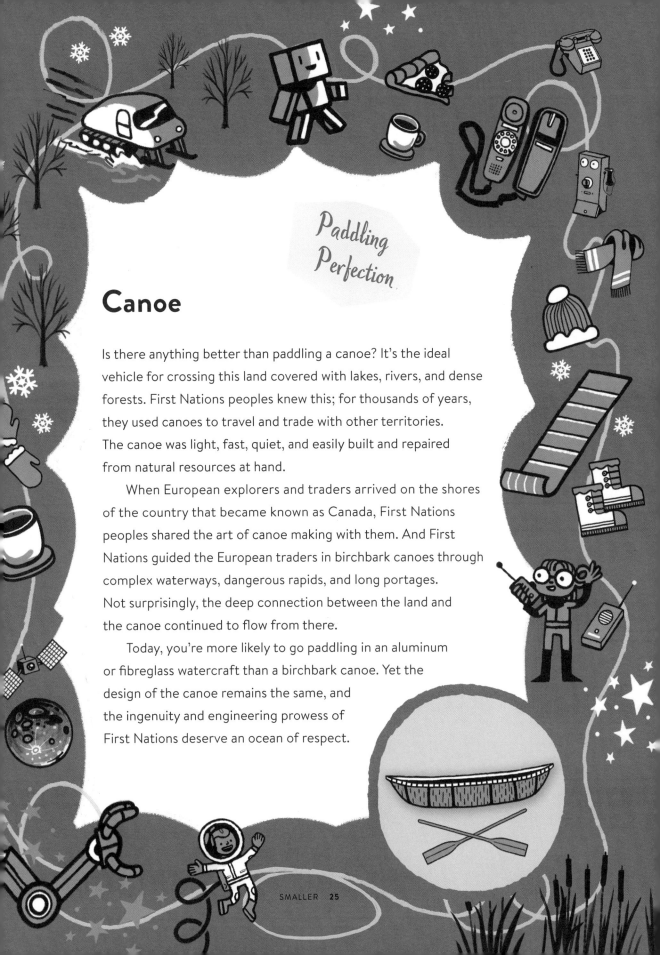

Paddling Perfection

Canoe

Is there anything better than paddling a canoe? It's the ideal vehicle for crossing this land covered with lakes, rivers, and dense forests. First Nations peoples knew this; for thousands of years, they used canoes to travel and trade with other territories. The canoe was light, fast, quiet, and easily built and repaired from natural resources at hand.

When European explorers and traders arrived on the shores of the country that became known as Canada, First Nations peoples shared the art of canoe making with them. And First Nations guided the European traders in birchbark canoes through complex waterways, dangerous rapids, and long portages. Not surprisingly, the deep connection between the land and the canoe continued to flow from there.

Today, you're more likely to go paddling in an aluminum or fibreglass watercraft than a birchbark canoe. Yet the design of the canoe remains the same, and the ingenuity and engineering prowess of First Nations deserve an ocean of respect.

Toboggan

For thousands of years, the First Nations peoples of Canada's Far North used toboggans for travel and to transport goods from place to place. The carefully designed vehicles were made to be pulled by people or dogs, and were long and narrow enough to slide within sled and snowshoe tracks. Built from larch and birch wood found in the area, the toboggan's front was curled up to make it easier to move through thick snow.

When European traders, hunters, and trappers arrived in Canada, they jumped on this transportation innovation. Soon the sport of downhill tobogganing took off at lightning speed, and tobogganing clubs and elaborate slides became fashionable. From this slippery trend grew new sports such as luge, bobsled, and skeleton—all of which are still popular Winter Olympic events.

Today in Canada's north, toboggans made of wood or plastic are often used with snowmobiles to transport goods and people. And, all across Canada, you'll find them speeding down a hill!

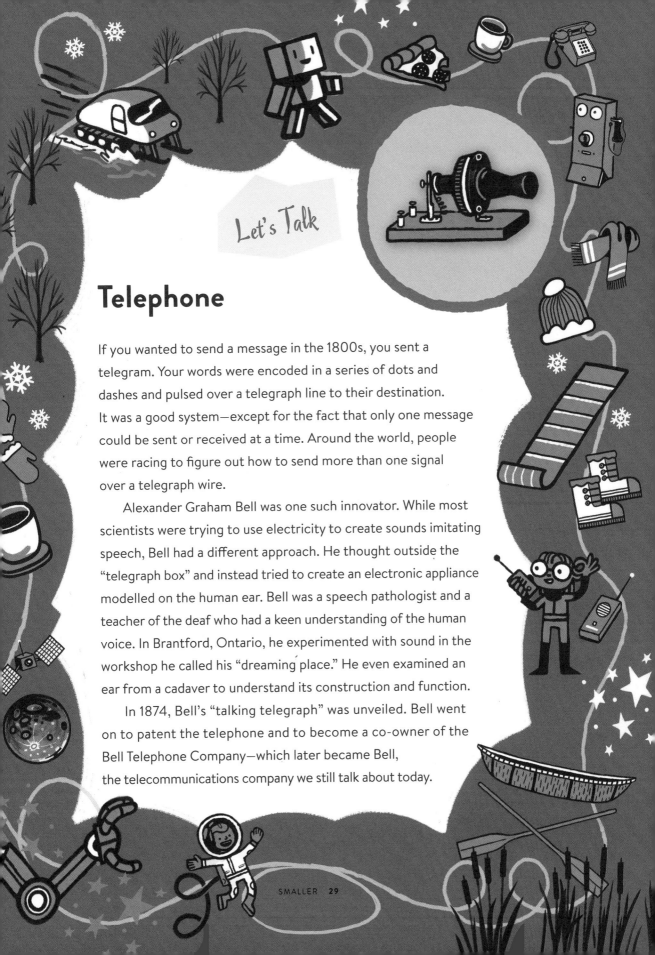

Let's Talk

Telephone

If you wanted to send a message in the 1800s, you sent a telegram. Your words were encoded in a series of dots and dashes and pulsed over a telegraph line to their destination. It was a good system—except for the fact that only one message could be sent or received at a time. Around the world, people were racing to figure out how to send more than one signal over a telegraph wire.

Alexander Graham Bell was one such innovator. While most scientists were trying to use electricity to create sounds imitating speech, Bell had a different approach. He thought outside the "telegraph box" and instead tried to create an electronic appliance modelled on the human ear. Bell was a speech pathologist and a teacher of the deaf who had a keen understanding of the human voice. In Brantford, Ontario, he experimented with sound in the workshop he called his "dreaming place." He even examined an ear from a cadaver to understand its construction and function.

In 1874, Bell's "talking telegraph" was unveiled. Bell went on to patent the telephone and to become a co-owner of the Bell Telephone Company—which later became Bell, the telecommunications company we still talk about today.

Snowmobile

A winter storm changed everything for Armand Bombardier, a mechanic who fixed cars and machines and sold gasoline at his garage in Valcourt, Quebec. One night in January 1934, a blizzard hit the town. Unfortunately, Bombardier's two-year-old son had an appendicitis attack the same night. At that time, most streets and roads in the town weren't ploughed. Bombardier couldn't get his son to the hospital in time, and the young boy died.

Bombardier set to work to build a vehicle that could travel in the snowiest and iciest conditions. In 1937, he introduced his first snowmobile, built to carry seven people. The snowmobile ran on a new sprocket wheel and track-drive system that Bombardier had invented.

Soon, the speedy snow machine was popular with doctors, ambulance drivers, priests, and others who needed to travel in harsh winter weather. Bombardier continued to innovate, and in 1959, he launched a miniature snowmobile—the first Ski-Doo—which is still hugely popular today. The company Bombardier founded went on to build subway cars, planes, and trains used around the world, and this father's legacy became a Canadian transportation legend.

Walkie-Talkie

"A Canadian built the first walkie-talkie. Do you copy?" Engineer and inventor Donald Hings created the wireless "packset" in 1937. He designed the portable two-way radio for bush pilots who had to fly between remote mining sites in Canada's Far North. Quickly, the handheld radio gained widespread use and became known as the walkie-talkie.

When the Second World War broke out in Europe two years later, Hings was summoned to Ottawa to adapt the walkie-talkie for the military. The device was sent to British, Canadian, and American troops and is credited with saving thousands of lives during the war.

After the war, the walkie-talkie became even more popular. Police officers, firefighters, paramedics, and truck drivers all used the device. The walkie-talkie even became a must-have for kids roaming around their neighbourhoods during the day and chatting under the covers late at night. "Time to go to sleep . . . Over and out."

Canadarm

When NASA needs a hand with their space program, Canada
doesn't refuse. In fact, in 1981, the Canadian engineers at SPAR
Aerospace built NASA a whole robotic arm. The Canadarm has
been an essential part of the U.S. space shuttle program for
more than thirty years. The Canadarm acts like a human arm—
with electric motors for muscles. A camera on its elbow acts as
an eye, and its joints are controlled by computers that act as a
brain. Astronauts have used the arm to repair equipment, launch
satellites, and move cargo—and even other astronauts.

Today, the second Canadarm can be found on the
International Space Station. In fact, two Canadarms worked
together to build the station. The arm on the shuttle handed
over pieces of the station to be assembled by the Canadarm
on the station. What do you call this space-age move?

Why, the "Canadian handshake," of course.

The Canadarm is also hard at work at home.
It is being used to develop tools to make
surgeries safer and easier. The sky's
the limit for Canadarm technology!

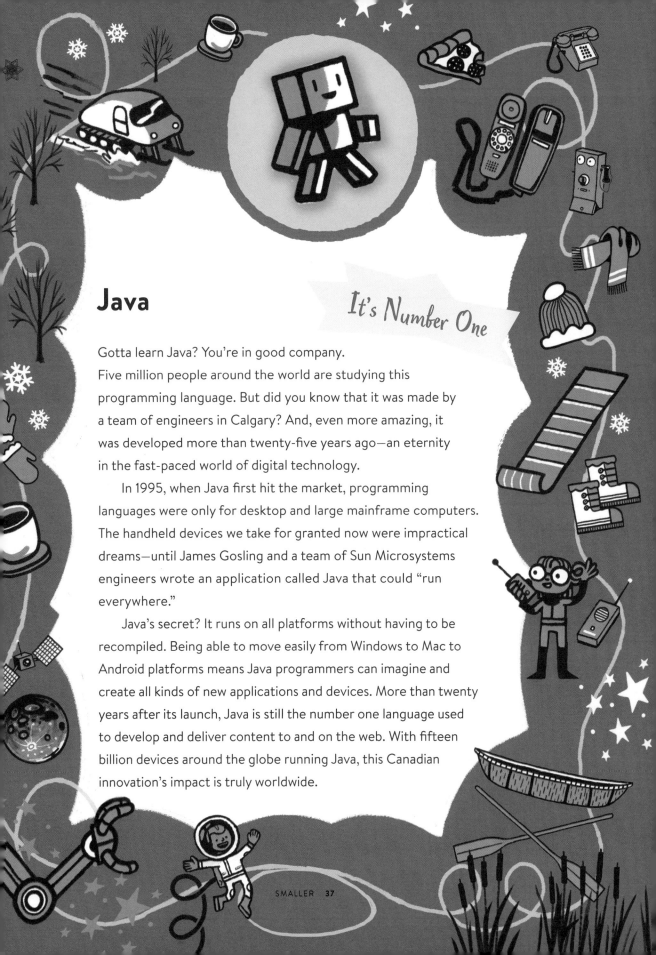

Java

Gotta learn Java? You're in good company. Five million people around the world are studying this programming language. But did you know that it was made by a team of engineers in Calgary? And, even more amazing, it was developed more than twenty-five years ago—an eternity in the fast-paced world of digital technology.

In 1995, when Java first hit the market, programming languages were only for desktop and large mainframe computers. The handheld devices we take for granted now were impractical dreams—until James Gosling and a team of Sun Microsystems engineers wrote an application called Java that could "run everywhere."

Java's secret? It runs on all platforms without having to be recompiled. Being able to move easily from Windows to Mac to Android platforms means Java programmers can imagine and create all kinds of new applications and devices. More than twenty years after its launch, Java is still the number one language used to develop and deliver content to and on the web. With fifteen billion devices around the globe running Java, this Canadian innovation's impact is truly worldwide.

How Canadian Innovators Made the World
KINDER

Canadians want a country that is both smart and caring. While trying to find better ways of treating each other, our innovators have quietly made the world a kinder place. From protecting human rights to developing electric wheelchairs that help people with disabilities be independent, Canadian innovation shows us that it's good to be kind.

Longhouse

Think it's hard to share a room with your brothers and sisters? Try sharing a house with sixteen other families. That's what the Haudenosaunee, Huron-Wendat, and other First Nations peoples did. They didn't just talk about community spirit—they lived it. For thousands of years, families from these First Nations shared living space in large structures called longhouses.

Yet, it wasn't just the idea of a building that reflected and nurtured cultural values of co-operation and collaboration that was so innovative. The actual construction of the longhouse was pretty cool, too. As many as 130 people could live in one large longhouse, which was divided into compartments for families. Two families slept in each compartment and shared a fire for cooking. To fit everyone in, people of all ages slept in bunk beds—another Haudenosaunee innovation that is now used around the world. To avoid wasted space, the roofs and ends of the buildings were rounded. New baby on the way? No need to move. The ends of the longhouse could be extended easily for growing families. For these communities, the longhouse was always home sweet home.

Forensic Pathology

Sure, superheroes are usually fighting crime in New York and other big cities. But do you know where else you could see exciting crime scene investigations? Saskatchewan, almost a hundred years ago.

In 1920, Dr. Frances McGill was Saskatchewan's chief pathologist. At that time, it was unusual for women to be medical doctors. It was even more unusual for a woman to be a pathologist. McGill's job was to study dead bodies to figure out the cause of death. She was the first person in Canada to make forensic crime science a regular part of police work. To investigate suspicious deaths, she would travel by dogsled and float plane throughout the large province to study crime scenes and protect and preserve evidence. McGill was a star in the courtroom as well. Her medical testimony was riveting to watch, rigorous in its detail and well known for saving the innocent and convicting the guilty.

Today, these pioneering crime scene methods are still used by police departments across Canada and around the world. Even in New York.

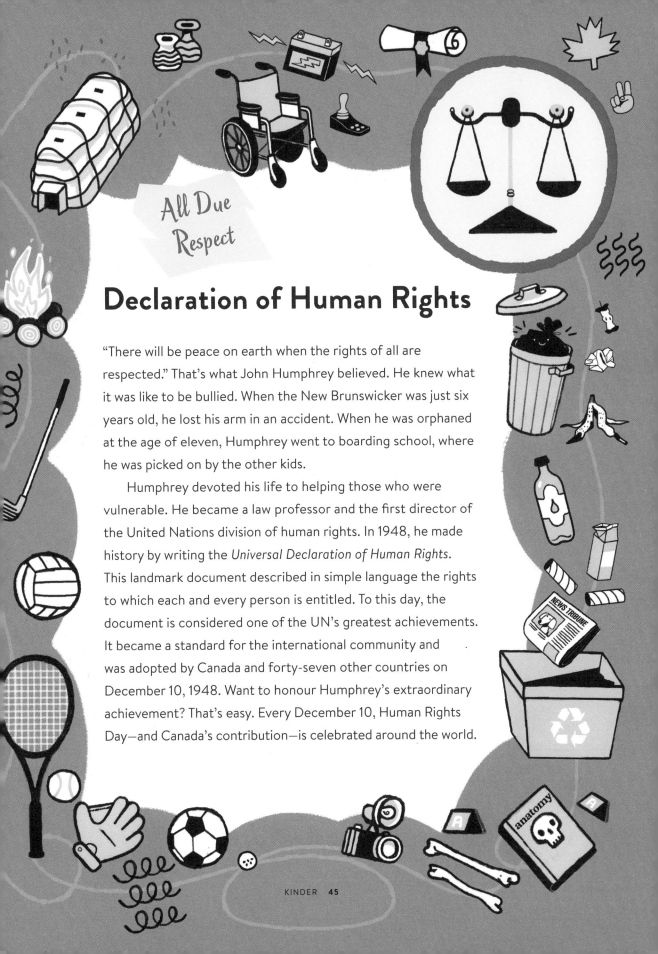

Declaration of Human Rights

"There will be peace on earth when the rights of all are respected." That's what John Humphrey believed. He knew what it was like to be bullied. When the New Brunswicker was just six years old, he lost his arm in an accident. When he was orphaned at the age of eleven, Humphrey went to boarding school, where he was picked on by the other kids.

Humphrey devoted his life to helping those who were vulnerable. He became a law professor and the first director of the United Nations division of human rights. In 1948, he made history by writing the *Universal Declaration of Human Rights*. This landmark document described in simple language the rights to which each and every person is entitled. To this day, the document is considered one of the UN's greatest achievements. It became a standard for the international community and was adopted by Canada and forty-seven other countries on December 10, 1948. Want to honour Humphrey's extraordinary achievement? That's easy. Every December 10, Human Rights Day—and Canada's contribution—is celebrated around the world.

Garbage Bag

It was the best of products, it was the worst of products . . . it was the garbage bag. In 1950, inventor Harry Wasylyk was looking for an alternative to the dirty, smelly metal garbage pails that were everywhere. Experimenting in his kitchen in Winnipeg, he came up with the idea for a garbage bag that was easy to use, clean, and surprisingly strong. Wasylyk sold his product to the Winnipeg General Hospital to line their metal pails. But the garbage bag really cleaned up when Union Carbide bought the invention and started selling bags for home use. Soon, they were found in homes around the world.

Fast forward twenty years, and millions—maybe even billions—of these indestructible garbage bags were piling up in landfill sites around the world. Luckily, another Canadian innovator came along to tackle this new problem. James Guillet was a "green" chemist who was experimenting to try to imitate natural processes like photosynthesis in his laboratory. He figured out how to create plastics that decompose in the sun. Thanks to Guillet and his handy biodegradable garbage bag, the landfill problem is being reduced.

Electric Wheelchair

The consequences of war last long after the conflict has ended. During the Second World War, many soldiers were gravely injured by bomb blasts. Thanks to penicillin, they survived their injuries, but some returned home as paraplegics and quadriplegics. At that time, only manual wheelchairs were available, and the injured soldiers didn't have the strength or ability to operate them. So George Klein, the talented engineer at Canada's National Research Council who developed the snow classification system, set to work to create an electric wheelchair.

The electric machine that Klein created could be used indoors or outdoors for long stretches of time. The wheelchair's control stick was easy to use, designed like a joystick on a game console today. Veterans were able to climb steep inclines and turn sharply in tight spaces in their wheelchairs.

Klein's innovation improved veterans' lives, but it also started the whole field of rehabilitation engineering—using technology to help people with disabilities or injuries. The talented engineer went on to create many other innovations. Klein even came out of retirement to work on the Canadarm. Now that's innovation dedication.

Blue Box Recycling

Newspaper. Bottles. Plastic containers. Cans. Nyle Ludolph, a garbage collector in Kitchener, Ontario, was upset by the vast amounts of waste he saw heading to the landfill every day.

Determined to do his bit to reduce the amount of garbage he threw out, Ludolph started recycling and composting at home. In twelve months, he and his wife and son had produced only six bags of garbage. Inspired by his experience, he convinced his boss to get into recycling. In 1983, the first blue box program was rolled out to thirty-five thousand households in Kitchener. The bright blue boxes could easily be seen in the grass or snow, and blue is resistant to fading in the sun's damaging ultraviolet rays.

Ludolph's simple recycling idea spread quickly across Canada and throughout North America and the world. Countless tons of waste have been turned into new products all because this innovative garbage collector thought, "There's got to be a better way."

The Better Way

A Win-Win

Right To Play

Play isn't all fun and games. It's also how we learn and grow physically and emotionally. Unfortunately, for many kids in developing countries, play isn't a part of everyday life.

Speed skater Johann Olav Koss learned this when he visited war-torn Eritrea a few months before the 1994 Winter Olympics. There, he met a group of boys. One of the boys tied his shirt into a ball for him and his friends to play with. But when the boy had to leave, the game was over.

Koss didn't forget these kids. After winning three gold medals, he donated his Olympic bonus and asked other athletes to do the same. Then, Koss returned to Eritrea with a planeload of sports equipment. And he didn't stop there. In 2000, he founded Right To Play in Toronto. Today, the international development organization gives more than a million kids in Africa, Asia, the Middle East, and North America a chance to learn through play. By realizing his dream, Koss is helping others realize theirs. Now that's a real win-win situation.

How Canadian Innovators Made the World

SAFER

Life is a risky business. That's why Canadians have collaborated to keep us safe in everyday situations. From life jackets to screwdrivers to goalie masks, their contributions reduce the risks we face. Now that's a country that puts safety first!

Igloo

What's the perfect shelter for the freezing temperatures and icy winds in Canada's north? The igloo, of course. We don't know who invented this ingenious architecture, but we do know that it's been the traditional home and shelter of the Inuit peoples for thousands of years. The Inuit made igloos from the area's most abundant resource—snow. The cosy refuge could be built to any size but was usually designed for one family.

To make an igloo, blocks cut from hard-packed snow are placed in a circle to form the foundation. The signature dome shape—which helps the structure stay strong—is created by trimming and adding blocks to form a sloping spiral. When the final block is placed at the very top, the igloo is complete. Snow is also used as mortar to seal the cracks between the blocks. This prevents cold air from entering and warm air from escaping, which allows body heat to warm the structure. To create this marvel of engineering, all you need is snow, some tools, and a few hours. Oh, and a skilled igloo builder helps too.

Life Jacket

Canada's waters are cold . . . really, really cold. On the ocean coast or on inland lakes, keeping warm is as important as staying afloat. In fact, people often die more quickly from heat loss than from drowning.

Inuit whale hunters knew this. To stay safe, they made the first flotation devices. Known as spring-pelts, the clothing was sewn from sealskin or seal gut. If hunters fell into the frigid water, the waterproof clothes would help keep them dry and warm and help them to float until they could be rescued. Over time, waterproof vests developed and became better and better at keeping people afloat and preventing the loss of body heat. Eventually, they evolved into the Personal Flotation Devices we know today. Of course, there is one catch to this life-saving innovation: a life jacket only works if you wear it!

The Fishers' Friend

Foghorn

The lower a sound is, the farther that sound can be heard to travel. That's just science. When an engineer in Saint John, New Brunswick, tuned in to that fact, he used it to save lives at sea.

One foggy night in 1853, Robert Foulis was walking home when he heard his daughter playing the piano. As the notes drifted through the dense fog, he noticed that he could hear the lowest notes most clearly. Foulis immediately realized how this discovery could benefit his community.

Fog made sea travel very dangerous on the East Coast. Lighthouse beams could not be seen in the fog, and ships were at risk of crashing into rocky shores—until Foulis developed the steam foghorn. The device was a megaphone that sent out codes made up of long, low notes. Whatever the weather conditions, these deep blasts could warn sailors of dangers close to shore. Although Foulis never made any money from the foghorn, his innovation earned him a place in maritime history. To this day, sailors and fishers are all ears for this life-saving idea.

Robertson Screwdriver

You could call it a happy accident. In 1908, Peter Robertson, a tool salesman from Milton, Ontario, was on a sales call in Montreal. He was demonstrating how to use a screwdriver to fasten slotted screws when the screwdriver slipped, badly cutting his hand. Robertson didn't get angry. He got inspired. Once his hand healed, he began to work on creating a safer screwdriver.

Robertson designed a screw and screwdriver that were an ideal match. The pyramid-shaped tip of the screwdriver fit exactly into the square indentation in the screw. This perfect pairing meant that Robertson's metal fastener could be screwed in faster, easier, and tighter than the old slotted version.

Immediately, Robertson's innovation was a hit. Henry Ford, the car manufacturer, started using Robertson screws and screwdrivers on his assembly lines. Thanks to the Robertson, each car could be built two hours faster. Today, more than a century later, the company Robertson started is still producing the superior square-drive screws.

Gas Mask

Fighting Back

When you're fighting in a war, anything can happen. In 1915, during the First World War, the German army used poison gas against Canadian and French troops. The only protection soldiers had was to breathe through fabric soaked in urine. (The urine crystallized the gas.) Dr. Cluny MacPherson, a medical officer from St. John's, Newfoundland, was caring for Canadian and other Allied troops. (Newfoundland didn't become part of Canada until 1949.) Concerned about the effect the gas was having on soldiers, MacPherson acted quickly to come up with a solution.

Inspired by the breathing masks used in deep sea diving, he created a canvas hood that completely covered the soldier's head. He attached the hood to a helmet taken from a captured German soldier and added eyepieces and a breathing tube. To absorb chlorine, the deadly element in the gas, MacPherson treated the mask with chemicals. His makeshift mask design became standard issue for soldiers, protecting countless men from death, blindness, burns, and other internal injuries. Millions of soldiers around the world still rely on the gas mask for protection today.

Shrouded Tuyere

Archimedes is not the only scientist to have a "eureka moment" in the bath. Montreal metallurgist Robert Lee also came up with an explosive idea in the tub. As a metallurgist, his job was to figure out the best way to combine metals to produce new materials. In 1958, steel was made by physically stirring iron, coal, and other elements together in a furnace. It was a very dangerous and inefficient process. Workers had to stir the hot liquid steel, and sometimes they got splashed and burned.

Lee knew there had to be a better way. One day, while relaxing in the bath, he found the answer. Lee tooted in the tub, and the bubbles of gas that appeared gave him an idea. He could use hot air to mix the steel. Lee developed the shrouded tuyere to blast hot air into the bottom of the furnace. As the air rose, it mixed the steel. Lee's bath-time brainwave went beyond improving safety and productivity in Canada; the shrouded tuyere is now used around the world. Eureka!

The Steel Stirrer

Goalie Mask

Today, hockey goalies have a lot of
equipment. But that wasn't always the case.
Fifty years ago, goalies didn't even wear masks. Luckily for
puckstoppers' faces everywhere, Montreal Canadiens goaltender
Jacques Plante changed that.

Plante was hit in the face in a game against the New York
Rangers in 1959. He was forced to leave the ice and have the
large gash stitched up. Afterward, Plante said he would only
return to the game if he could wear the white fibreglass mask
he'd made to protect his face during practice. His coach
said no; he didn't want one of his players to look like a coward.
But the star insisted, saying, "Let me play wearing my mask
or I don't play at all."

Plante skated back onto the ice wearing his fibreglass mask.
Plante and the Canadiens went on to win the game, and the
Stanley Cup that season. The hockey innovator kept wearing the
mask and became a hero and role model to all future players.
Now there's a real game changer.

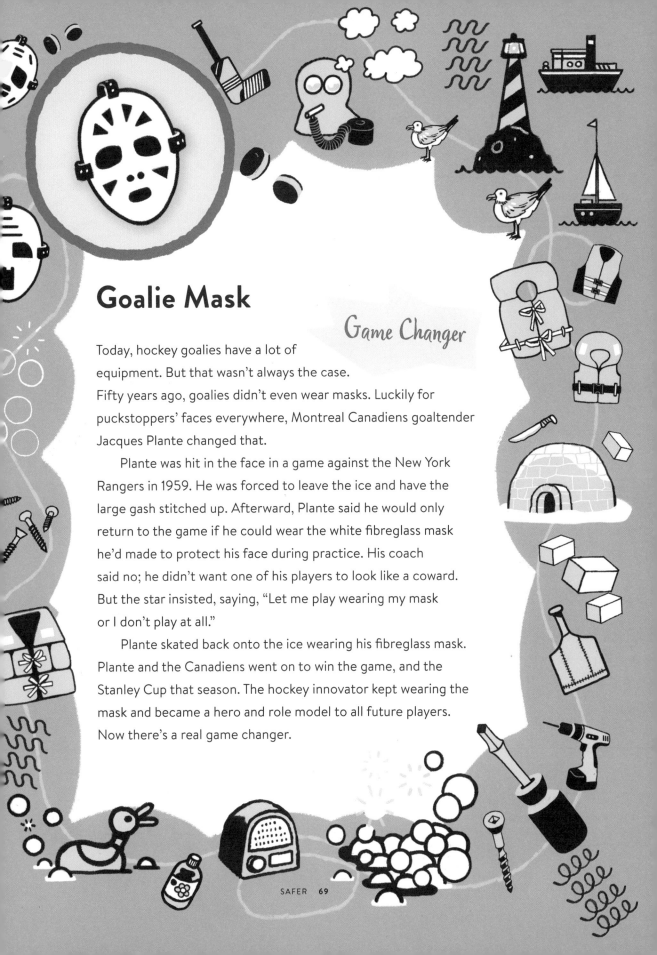

How Canadian
Innovators Made the World
HEALTHIER

When you have your health,
you have everything. Canadians
in hospitals, research labs,
and universities across the
country are working to find
cures and treatments. With
breakthroughs such as the
discovery of insulin and tech-
savvy telesurgery, the world is in
better shape thanks to Canada.

Peanut Butter

Crunchy or creamy? Whichever your preference, you probably agree that peanut butter is a glorious snack for the allergy-free. So who's to thank for this stick-to-the-roof-of-your-mouth treat? A Canadian, of course.

Marcellus Gilmore Edson was a chemist living in Quebec. When he was grinding peanuts, he discovered that if he heated the grinding surfaces, the crushed peanuts became a thick, chunky fluid. After the fluid cooled, it turned into a paste similar to butter. Edson saw the promise in his paste. He named the tasty treat peanut-candy and patented the product in 1884.

When John Kellogg, a doctor in Michigan and the founder of the Kellogg cereal empire, heard about peanut-candy he got stuck on an idea. Kellogg bought up the peanut spread and advertised it as a protein substitute for people who couldn't eat solid food. Appreciation for the nutritious and delicious snack spread. Today, it's still the favourite ingredient in PB&J sandwiches everywhere. Crushed it.

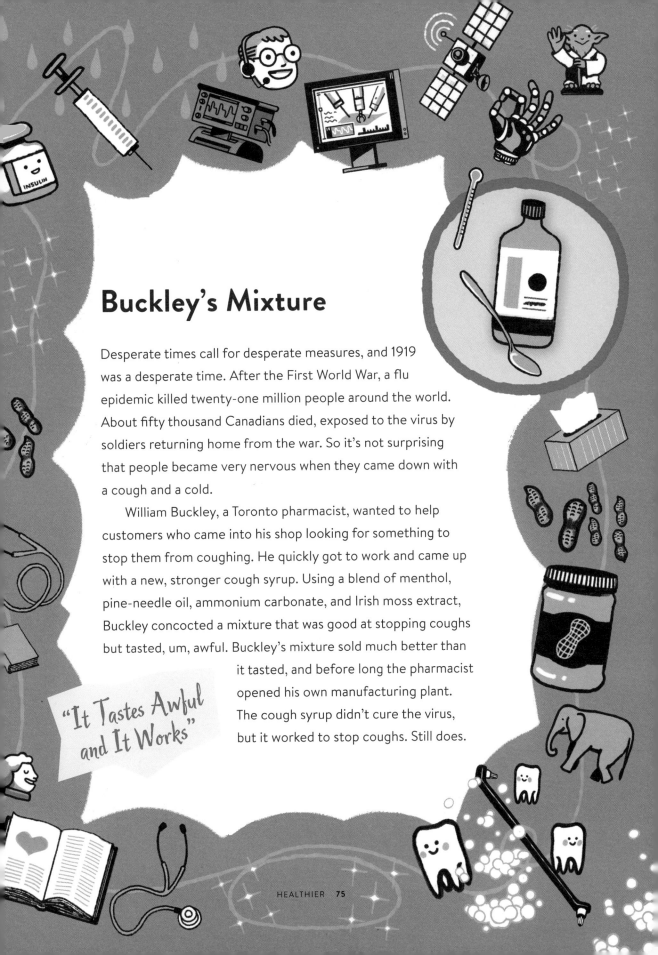

Buckley's Mixture

Desperate times call for desperate measures, and 1919 was a desperate time. After the First World War, a flu epidemic killed twenty-one million people around the world. About fifty thousand Canadians died, exposed to the virus by soldiers returning home from the war. So it's not surprising that people became very nervous when they came down with a cough and a cold.

William Buckley, a Toronto pharmacist, wanted to help customers who came into his shop looking for something to stop them from coughing. He quickly got to work and came up with a new, stronger cough syrup. Using a blend of menthol, pine-needle oil, ammonium carbonate, and Irish moss extract, Buckley concocted a mixture that was good at stopping coughs but tasted, um, awful. Buckley's mixture sold much better than it tasted, and before long the pharmacist opened his own manufacturing plant. The cough syrup didn't cure the virus, but it worked to stop coughs. Still does.

"It Tastes Awful and It Works"

Insulin

Diabetes used to be a deadly disease. That is, until Canadian doctors Frederick Banting, Charles Best, and their University of Toronto adviser J.J.R. Macleod set out to find a cure. At the time, doctors knew that the pancreas released a substance to control the amount of glucose (sugar) in the blood. However, when a person had diabetes, the body couldn't control the glucose, and the patient became ill. Even worse, doctors didn't know how to treat the condition.

Banting and Best launched a series of experiments to solve the mystery of the disease. In the summer of 1921, they discovered the hormone that controls glucose levels—what we now know as insulin. Joined by biochemist James Collip, they were able to create insulin that was a reliable remedy for the dreaded disease. With the help of the drug firm Eli Lilly and Company, large quantities of insulin were produced and the treatment became widely available.

Insulin was a miracle of modern medicine. Gravely ill people were saved by the wonder drug. Now, thanks to these collaborative Canadians, people all over the world with diabetes stay strong.

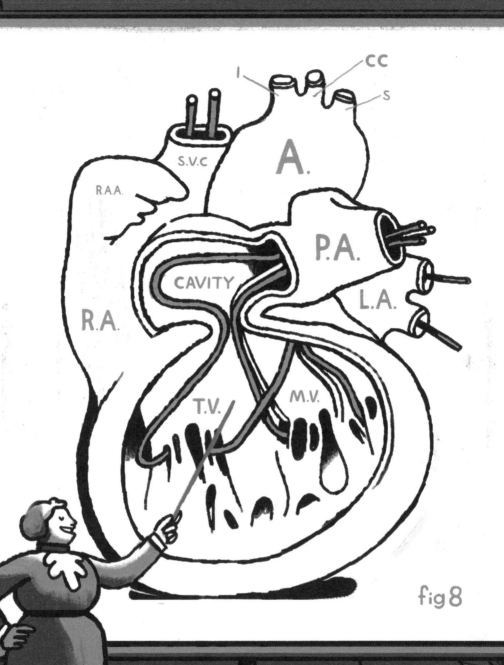

fig 8

Atlas of the Heart

To fix something, you first need to understand what's wrong with it. So to have any hope of repairing a damaged heart, you first must know all the different things that can go wrong with this important organ. Maude Abbott, a medical pathologist, knew this. She used her position as the assistant curator of McGill University Medical Museum to collect and study the hearts of people who had died of heart problems. For years she scoured medical records and compiled information from autopsies to become a world expert on heart disease and heart defects.

In 1936, Abbott published her research in a document called *The Atlas of Congenital Cardiac Disease*. For the first time, heart surgeons had a comprehensive reference to diagnose and treat their patients' heart problems. What makes Maude Abbott's accomplishment even more heart-stopping is the sexism she faced throughout her career. Because she was a woman, Abbott wasn't allowed to go to McGill's medical school in 1889. After her remarkable achievements, the university saw the error of its ways and awarded her a medical degree in 1936. Call it a long overdue change of heart.

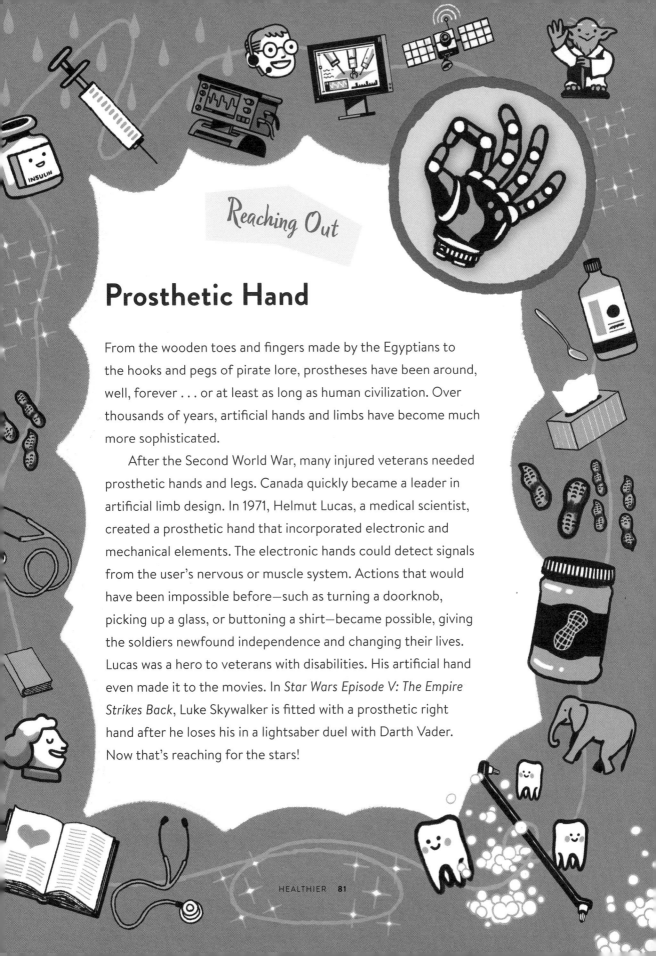

Reaching Out

Prosthetic Hand

From the wooden toes and fingers made by the Egyptians to the hooks and pegs of pirate lore, prostheses have been around, well, forever . . . or at least as long as human civilization. Over thousands of years, artificial hands and limbs have become much more sophisticated.

After the Second World War, many injured veterans needed prosthetic hands and legs. Canada quickly became a leader in artificial limb design. In 1971, Helmut Lucas, a medical scientist, created a prosthetic hand that incorporated electronic and mechanical elements. The electronic hands could detect signals from the user's nervous or muscle system. Actions that would have been impossible before—such as turning a doorknob, picking up a glass, or buttoning a shirt—became possible, giving the soldiers newfound independence and changing their lives. Lucas was a hero to veterans with disabilities. His artificial hand even made it to the movies. In *Star Wars Episode V: The Empire Strikes Back*, Luke Skywalker is fitted with a prosthetic right hand after he loses his in a lightsaber duel with Darth Vader. Now that's reaching for the stars!

Sulcabrush

Wisdom for Teeth

Brush, brush, brush your teeth morning, noon, and night . . .
While this little ditty offers good advice, Canadian dentist
Dr. Max Florence knew that typical teethbrushing can't clean
between your teeth or along the gum line, no matter how
dedicated the brusher. To tackle the problem, Florence did some
research—some ancient research. He knew that other brushing
tools have been used for thousands of years, including neem-
tree twigs in India and miswaks through the Horn of Africa. By
chewing neem sticks and miswaks, people could clean between
teeth and along sensitive gum lines. But because the bristles
on these sticks stood straight out, it was impossible to clean
behind the back teeth.

So in 1985, Florence came up with a new hybrid brush
that had bristles at both ends. The bristles are long, pointed,
and angled in different directions. This simple innovation
made it easy to improve teeth-cleaning and treat
gum disease. Thirty years later, Florence's
Sulcabrush is still the one dentists routinely
recommend. Who's smiling now?

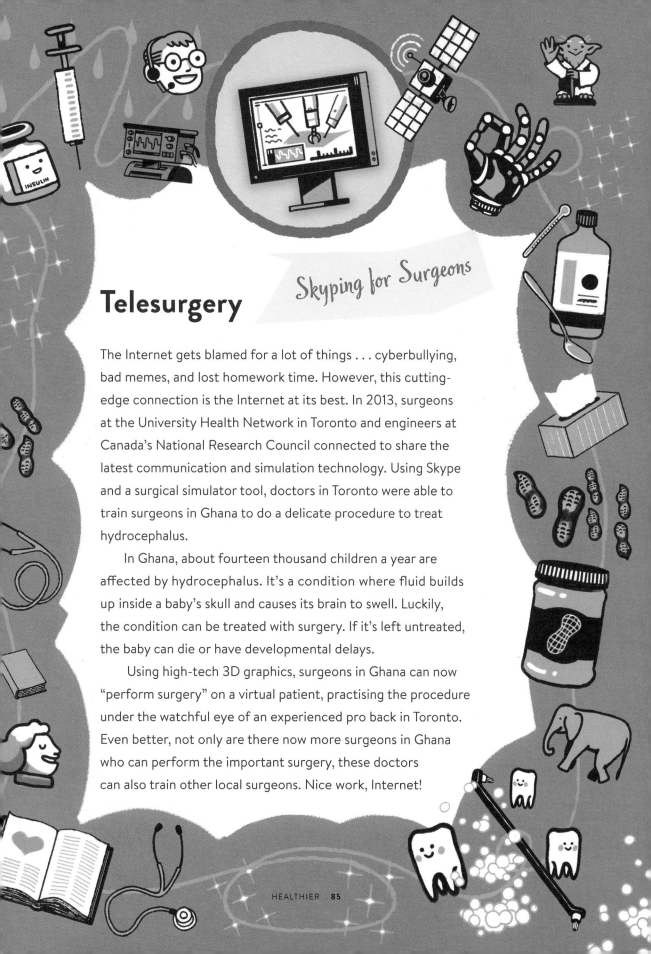

Telesurgery

Skyping for Surgeons

The Internet gets blamed for a lot of things . . . cyberbullying, bad memes, and lost homework time. However, this cutting-edge connection is the Internet at its best. In 2013, surgeons at the University Health Network in Toronto and engineers at Canada's National Research Council connected to share the latest communication and simulation technology. Using Skype and a surgical simulator tool, doctors in Toronto were able to train surgeons in Ghana to do a delicate procedure to treat hydrocephalus.

In Ghana, about fourteen thousand children a year are affected by hydrocephalus. It's a condition where fluid builds up inside a baby's skull and causes its brain to swell. Luckily, the condition can be treated with surgery. If it's left untreated, the baby can die or have developmental delays.

Using high-tech 3D graphics, surgeons in Ghana can now "perform surgery" on a virtual patient, practising the procedure under the watchful eye of an experienced pro back in Toronto. Even better, not only are there now more surgeons in Ghana who can perform the important surgery, these doctors can also train other local surgeons. Nice work, Internet!

How Canadian Innovators Made the World

WEALTHIER

Innovative ideas transform industries, helping businesses to grow and the country to prosper. Whether with a chocolate bar to eat on the go or an IMAX theatre transforming the film industry, Canada has proved that innovation itself is the new wealth of nations.

Canada Dry

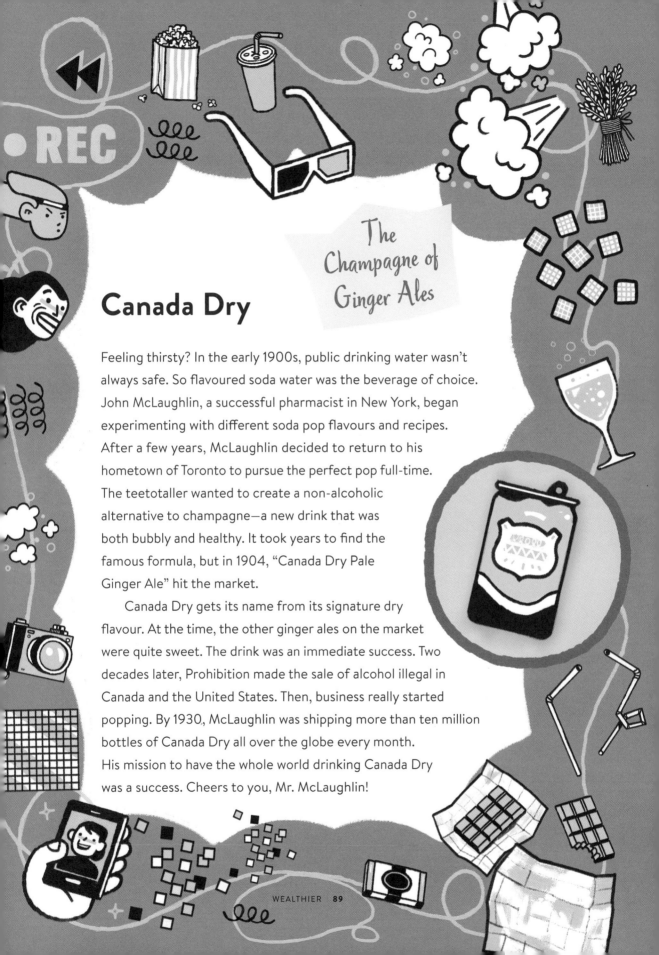

The
Champagne of
Ginger Ales

Feeling thirsty? In the early 1900s, public drinking water wasn't always safe. So flavoured soda water was the beverage of choice. John McLaughlin, a successful pharmacist in New York, began experimenting with different soda pop flavours and recipes. After a few years, McLaughlin decided to return to his hometown of Toronto to pursue the perfect pop full-time. The teetotaller wanted to create a non-alcoholic alternative to champagne—a new drink that was both bubbly and healthy. It took years to find the famous formula, but in 1904, "Canada Dry Pale Ginger Ale" hit the market.

Canada Dry gets its name from its signature dry flavour. At the time, the other ginger ales on the market were quite sweet. The drink was an immediate success. Two decades later, Prohibition made the sale of alcohol illegal in Canada and the United States. Then, business really started popping. By 1930, McLaughlin was shipping more than ten million bottles of Canada Dry all over the globe every month. His mission to have the whole world drinking Canada Dry was a success. Cheers to you, Mr. McLaughlin!

Chocolate Bar

The Travelling Treat

Want to hear a great fishing story? It's the sweet tale of two New Brunswick chocolatiers who left work for an afternoon of fishing. As they gathered their gear, Arthur Ganong (president of his family's chocolate company) and George Ensor (its superintendent) slipped chunks of chocolate in their pockets for a snack. No surprise, the treat was delicious. But it left them with messy hands and messier pockets. So on their next fishing trip, they wrapped their snack in a protective wrapper that repelled liquids, including melted chocolate.

That's when George and Arthur started to taste the possibilities. They enjoyed this travelling treat. Why shouldn't everyone? So in the summer of 1910, the Ganong company in St. Stephen began to make a two-piece wrapped chocolate bar. Five generations of Ganongs later, the company located in what's now officially known as Canada's chocolate town continues its tradition of sweet success.

Whoopee Cushion

Gags and prank items were all the rage in the 1920s. From a child's scream to a cat's screech, people couldn't get enough of goofy toys that made strange sounds for playing pranks. In this crowded and noisy market, one toy's timeless sound rang out clearer than the rest: the Whoopee Cushion.

The Whoopee Cushion—one of the most famous toys of all time—was discovered by accident. Some employees at the JEM Rubber Company in Toronto were experimenting with sheets of rubber and happened upon a distinct sound. It was music to their prank-loving ears, and they got to work to create the rootin' tootin' rubber pillow. An American novelty-sales business named Johnson Smith & Company added JEM's doohickey to its giant joke catalogue. Soon pranksters all across the United States and Canada were using the windy blaster to surprise, embarrass, and have a laugh with their friends and families. To this day, the Whoopee Cushion is one the world's top-selling novelty items. Remember that the next time someone offers you a chair.

The Windy Blaster

Shreddies

What's so special about Shreddies? More than you might guess. For starters, this crunchy confection was made for the first time in Niagara Falls, Ontario, more than seventy-five years ago by Nabisco. At that time, Shreddies was a revolution in breakfast cereals. The bite-sized bits were the only cereal made from whole-grain wheat knitted together like threads. Plus, the natural, sweet malt taste earned it the slogan "the breakfast cereal for kids that even a mother can love."

When Shreddies was first released, sales in Canada were slow. However, across the pond in the United Kingdom, the cereal quickly became a breakfast favourite. Today, you'll find the breakfast classic on grocery store shelves in both countries. So whether you see diamonds or squares floating in your bowl, eat up. This whole-wheat treat is still a whole lot of fun.

Diamonds or Squares?

Instant Replay

Ever heard of George Retzlaff? Probably not, but he is one of the most important people in the history of sports. As the producer of *Hockey Night in Canada*, Retzlaff was in charge of putting together the TV broadcast for the Saturday night faceoff. Retzlaff worked hard to make sure fans at home could follow the action on the ice. Yet sometimes viewers could barely see the puck on their TV screen. So Retzlaff came up with an idea. In 1955, he recorded a goal and then replayed it later. When videotape technology was invented the next year, replays of the most amazing moments of the game became a regular feature of the show.

Soon the instant replay became a standard feature of sports broadcasts around the world. TV viewers could get another peek at a home run, a slam dunk, or a hundred metre dash. Instant video replay changed sports—from the way games are played to how fans watch. These days, even referees use it as a tool during the games. Now that's a sports innovation story worth repeating!

Fan Fave

Digital Photography

"Come up with something new." That's what William Boyle's boss told him one day in 1969. The Nova Scotia native was working at Bell Laboratories when he got that simple instruction. So Boyle got to work, and fast.

In just one afternoon, Boyle came up with the idea of a "charge-coupled device." What's that, you ask? Well, it was the "something new" his boss wanted—the tech that lets us take photos with our cell phones. A charge-coupled device takes light particles and converts them into electric info that can be seen on our digital devices. Although Boyle came up with the idea for digital photography in a flash, it took a team of experts years to make his vision a reality. Next time you take out your smartphone for a selfie, give a silent shout-out to William Boyle and his pals for bringing digital photography to (your) life.

The Selfie Story

IMAX

Moviegoers want to see something extraordinary. Going to the theatre gives us what watching flicks at home just can't. The glow of the big screen is part of what makes the movies special.

Today, nothing delivers the big-screen experience quite like IMAX. Created in 1971 by five guys in Toronto, the IMAX motion picture projection system wasn't just about the super-sized screen. It was an important innovation in film technology, creating a whole new movie-going experience. Together, Ron Jones, William Shaw, Roman Kroitor, Robert Kerr, and Graeme Ferguson worked on a way to project super-sized film stock that was so large its picture would fill a viewer's field of vision. By running the large film sideways in a rolling loop, they were able to give audiences a steadier, clearer—and most of all—bigger experience in theatres. Up to ten times bigger, to be exact. Surrounded by the curved screen and immersed in pitch-perfect sound, watching an IMAX movie is as close to reality as you can get on the big screen. That's technology that sees the big picture.

How Canadian Innovators Made the World
HAPPIER

Some innovations make us feel better. The taste of maple syrup. The excitement of a Stanley Cup final game. The thrill of a Cirque du Soleil show. Thanks to the creativity of Canadians and their innovations, the world is a much happier place.

Maple Syrup

When you pour a generous serving of maple syrup over your stack of pancakes, you're tapping into a long tradition. The First Nations living in eastern Canada were the first people to recognize the sweet goodness of maple sap. For countless generations, they collected sap from red, sugar, and black maple trees in late winter and early spring. They understood its value as a source of energy and nutrients, drinking maple sap and using it in cooking. They also made maple syrup. To evaporate the water from the sap, they placed stones heated in a fire in pots of sap.

Over the last several hundred years, new tools and processes have been introduced to speed up the evaporation process and improve the syrup quality. Today, the spring ritual is big business. Canada produces 80 per cent of the world's maple syrup. Our maple candies, maple butter, and maple sugar are also famous with sweet-loving diners around the globe—in all seasons!

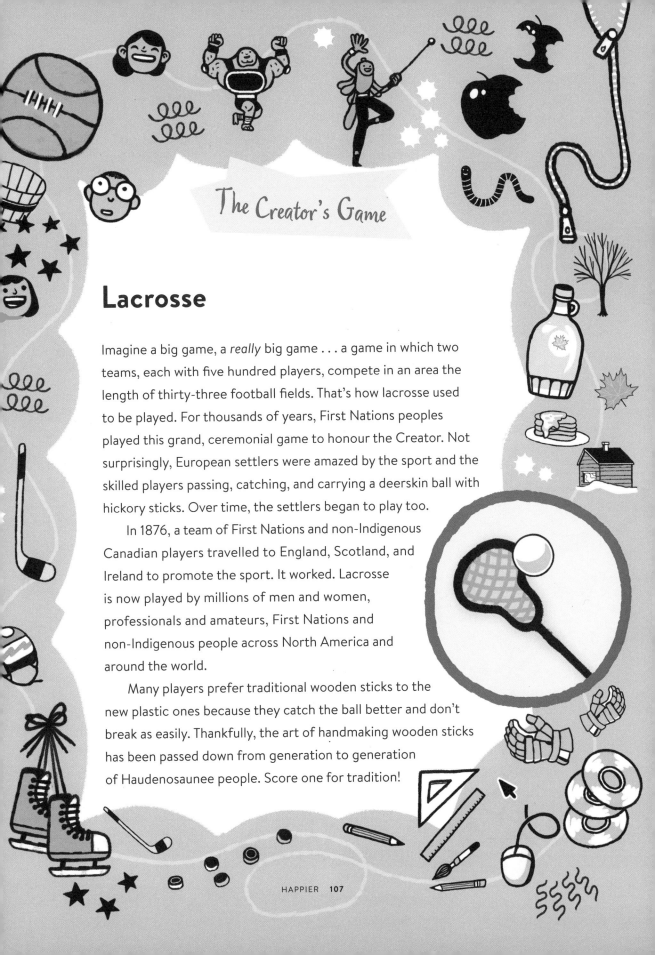

Lacrosse

Imagine a big game, a *really* big game . . . a game in which two teams, each with five hundred players, compete in an area the length of thirty-three football fields. That's how lacrosse used to be played. For thousands of years, First Nations peoples played this grand, ceremonial game to honour the Creator. Not surprisingly, European settlers were amazed by the sport and the skilled players passing, catching, and carrying a deerskin ball with hickory sticks. Over time, the settlers began to play too.

In 1876, a team of First Nations and non-Indigenous Canadian players travelled to England, Scotland, and Ireland to promote the sport. It worked. Lacrosse is now played by millions of men and women, professionals and amateurs, First Nations and non-Indigenous people across North America and around the world.

Many players prefer traditional wooden sticks to the new plastic ones because they catch the ball better and don't break as easily. Thankfully, the art of handmaking wooden sticks has been passed down from generation to generation of Haudenosaunee people. Score one for tradition!

McIntosh Apple

From humble beginnings come great things. One day in 1811, John McIntosh was clearing some land on his farm in eastern Ontario when he spotted a sapling. He'd never seen anything like it—apple trees didn't grow wild in the Canadian bush. McIntosh cared for the tree until it produced, you guessed it, the first McIntosh apples. Every crisp McIntosh you've ever eaten is a direct descendent of this little sapling.

McIntosh and his family got to work breeding the tree. The cold nights and clear autumn days in the region offered the perfect growing conditions for the fruit. The family expanded their business in 1879, shipping apples across eastern Canada and to the northeastern United States. Ideal for both cooking and eating, the McIntosh continues to grow in popularity in North America and Europe.

An Inspiring Fruit

This fruit really *is* inspiring. Steve Jobs, a lover of natural foods, chose Apple as the name for his famous computer company. Then, in 1984, employee Jef Raskin named the first personal computer after his fave apple—the McIntosh. Sure, it's spelled Macintosh, but for Canadians it will always be the apple of our eye.

Hockey

Strap on your skates and grab your sticks. It's time to hit the ice and celebrate. March 3 is not a national holiday, but many hockey fans think it should be. That day in 1875, students from McGill University gathered in Montreal to play the first indoor ice hockey game.

Hockey had been played informally many times before, both in Canada and Great Britain. In fact, games in which players wield curved sticks to whack a ball have been around since the days of Ancient Egypt. However, players strapping on sharpened steel blades to compete on ice in a cold building is a quintessentially Canadian innovation.

Many First Nations played an early version of ice hockey. Mi'kmaq teams competed in stick-and-ball matches on frozen lakes near what is now Dartmouth, Nova Scotia, in the 1740s. Their skates were made from animal jawbones strapped to their footwear with thongs of hide. So without a doubt, hockey has been a beloved winter sport for a long time. With our long, cold winters, it's no surprise our national game would leave it all on the ice.

Basketball

Sometimes you have to jump through hoops for your boss. James Naismith did. In 1891, he was teaching physical education at the YMCA training school in Springfield, Massachusetts. When winter came and the class couldn't play the usual outdoor sports, his boss asked him to come up with a new game.

At first, Naismith tried to adapt soccer, football, and lacrosse for the indoor gym, but nothing worked. So he thought back to his own childhood growing up in a small town outside of Ottawa. He remembered a game he and his friends played, throwing stones at a target. Naismith decided to try adapting it for the teens. Since the group was large, he divided the class into two teams and gave them a leather ball to throw instead of stones. Peach baskets nailed high above the ground became the targets. Not only did Naismith make his boss and students happy, he scored with future basketball players around the world. Today, millions of people in dozens of countries play and watch b-ball, and Naismith's legacy is a slam dunk.

Hoop Dreams

Letting It Slide

Zipper

Imagine life without zippers. How would you close your backpack? Do up your jacket? Check to see if you were flying low? Sometimes the innovations that have the biggest impact on our lives don't do grand things. Like the zipper, they just make our day-to-day actions easier and faster, and our lives a bit better.

Gideon Sundback, a Swedish-born electrical engineer, got the zipper on track after being hired to work for a fastener company. In 1913, he came up with the Hookless No. 2 to replace the time-consuming buckles and hooks and eyes found on clothing. Sundback's creation is the metal zipper we know today, those handy strips of teeth latched together by pulling up on a slider.

Sundback also created a machine to manufacture the fastener, and production started rolling in St. Catharines, Ontario. But sales were slow. When the B.F. Goodrich Company introduced the Zipper Boot in 1923, the new fastener finally caught on. By the Second World War, zippers were everywhere. Now that satisfying *zip* is heard around the world.

Superman

It's a bird! It's a plane! It's Superman! Sure, you see him everywhere now—comics, movies, TV, novels, even a Broadway show. But until 1933, Superman didn't even exist. In fact, no superhero did. Joe Shuster, a Toronto artist, and his writing partner Jerry Seigel were the first to create a comic book superhero.

Despite Superman's amazing powers (super-strength, flight, super speed, heat vision, freeze breath, X-ray vision, superhuman hearing, invulnerability), or maybe because of these cutting-edge capabilities, the duo had a hard time getting their story published. Finally, after nearly six years of rejection, Superman stepped out of the telephone booth in Action Comics No. 1 in June 1938. For just ten cents, fans could read about the crime-fighting superhero. By the next year, their Man of Steel had his own series and was selling more than half a million copies per month. Today, superheroes are just as popular as ever. Shuster's first Superman comic sold for $3.2 million at auction. Great Krypton! That's a super return on a ten-cent investment.

Cirque du Soleil

Reinventing the Circus

Simply breathtaking. That's the only way to describe Cirque du Soleil. The Montreal-based company started by stilt-walker Gilles Ste-Croix and fire-breather Guy Laliberté in 1984 didn't try to compete with old-style spectacles like Ringling Bros. and Barnum & Bailey. It set out to reinvent the circus. Every Cirque show has a different theme and its own dramatic storyline. While Cirque kept the tent, the clowns, and the classic acrobats of traditional circuses, they used them in a bold, new way. Enchanting illusions, wild, colourful costumes, and gravity-defying feats keep audiences riveted and coming back. By the 1990s, the stunning show was playing to sold-out crowds across Canada and in the United States and Europe.

Over its four-decade history, this creative Canadian company has become the largest theatrical producer in the world. From twenty street performers, Cirque du Soleil has grown to a company of four thousand employees. The spellbinding circus has performed for more than 180 million spectators in over sixty countries on six continents and its audience continues to grow. Imaginative and innovative, Cirque du Soleil has earned its moment in the sun.

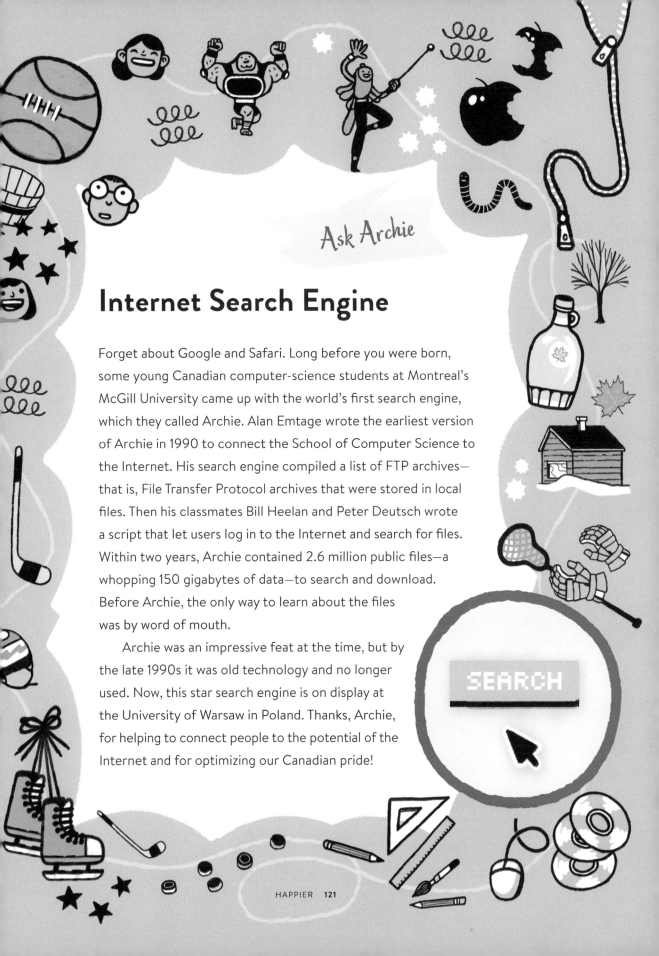

Ask Archie

Internet Search Engine

Forget about Google and Safari. Long before you were born, some young Canadian computer-science students at Montreal's McGill University came up with the world's first search engine, which they called Archie. Alan Emtage wrote the earliest version of Archie in 1990 to connect the School of Computer Science to the Internet. His search engine compiled a list of FTP archives—that is, File Transfer Protocol archives that were stored in local files. Then his classmates Bill Heelan and Peter Deutsch wrote a script that let users log in to the Internet and search for files. Within two years, Archie contained 2.6 million public files—a whopping 150 gigabytes of data—to search and download. Before Archie, the only way to learn about the files was by word of mouth.

Archie was an impressive feat at the time, but by the late 1990s it was old technology and no longer used. Now, this star search engine is on display at the University of Warsaw in Poland. Thanks, Archie, for helping to connect people to the potential of the Internet and for optimizing our Canadian pride!

SEARCH

A TIMELINE OF

EARLY HISTORY

Canoe
Duck Decoy
Igloo
Lacrosse
Life Jacket
Longhouse
Maple Syrup
Toboggan

1800s

1811 McIntosh Apple
1853 Foghorn
1874 Light Bulb
Telephone
1875 Hockey
1884 Peanut Butter
1891 Basketball

1900s

1904 Canada Dry
1908 Robertson Screwdriver
1910 Chocolate Bar
1913 Zipper
1915 Gas Mask
1919 Buckley's Mixture
1920 Dump Truck
Forensic Pathology
1921 Insulin
1925 Electric Radio
1930 Whoopee Cushion
1933 Superman
1936 Atlas of the Heart
1937 Snowmobile
Walkie-Talkie
1939 Shreddies

INNOVATION

2000s

HOW YOU CAN

Inquire
Investigate Issues and Solutions

Ideate
Develop an Idea

- Investigate past innovations and present issues.

- What or who inspires you?

- What can you learn from past and present innovations?

- Imagine what your innovation looks like. What do you need to create it?

- Why is this innovation needed? What are the problems or issues that it addresses?

- Who can you work with to develop your idea—friends, family, classmates, parents, teachers, experts?

- How can you make connections with other ideas?

- How will you stay motivated when facing challenges?

- What impact do you want your innovation to have?

BE AN INNOVATOR

Incubate
Test and Revise Your Ideas

Implement
Put Your Innovation into Action

- What challenges are you facing?

- How will you test your innovation and make changes based on the feedback you receive?

- Are there different versions of the innovation that might work better?

- Is the innovation having the impact you wanted?

- What is your plan for making and promoting your innovation?

  - design
  - marketing
  - materials
  - budget
  - schedule

- What roles do other team members have?

- How can you protect your innovation idea?

- Do you need any other resources?

- Should you register your innovation?

- How will you measure your success?

ACKNOWLEDGMENTS

The authors wish to express their delight and appreciation for the expert advice of the many collaborators across Canada who made *Innovation Nation* possible. They include . . .

Maria Aubrey, Christine Balasch, Alex Benay, Guy Berthiaume, Derek Beselt, Cynthia Biasolo, Dick Bourgeois-Doyle, Catherine Campbell, Maria Cantalini-Williams, Joanne Charette, Elizabeth Chestney, Azka Choudhary, Lois Claxton, Annabelle Cloutier, Sandra Corbeil, Jenny Kay Dupuis, Stephen Downes, Joe Dwyer, Carol Elder, Guy Freedman, Chad Gaffield, Daniel Goldberg, Jean Paul Gladu, Scott Haldane, Brian Hanington, Brent Herbert-Copley, Kimberlee Hesas, Ted Hewitt, Josh Holinaty, Monique Horth, Piita Irniq, Lisa Jager, Caroline Jamet, Margaret Joyce, Joe Karetak, Carla Kean, Millie Knapp, Elizabeth Kribs, Mary Beth Leatherdale, Jean Lebel, Steven Leclair, Joe Lee, Hélène Létourneau, Laurie Maier, Soriana Mantini, Richard Mayne, Ryan McKay-Fleming, Craig McNaughton, Marcia Mordfield, André Morriseau, Duncan Mousseau, Nipissing University Faculty of Education, Sheila Noble, Andrew Norgaard, Pamela Osti, Gilles Patry, Doug Pepper, Luiza Pereira, Leanne Perreault, John Phillips, Sarah Prevette, Neil Randall, Tony Reinhart, Julie Rocheleau, Fiona Smith-Hale, Wilf Stefan, Renée Tremblay, Lahring Tribe, Margot Vanderlaan, Paul Wagner, Tara Walker, Stephen Wallace, Christopher Walters, Tonia Williams . . .

. . . and all the other creative souls whose thoughtful work brought this volume to life.

THE AUTHORS

One of Canada's most respected and beloved governors general, **DAVID JOHNSTON** is a graduate of Harvard, Cambridge, and Queen's universities. He served as dean of law at Western University, principal of McGill University, and president of the University of Waterloo. He is the author or co-author of twenty-five books, holds honorary doctorates from over twenty universities, and is a Companion of the Order of Canada (C.C.). Born in Sudbury, Ontario, he grew up in Sault Ste. Marie. He is married to Sharon Johnston and has five daughters and fourteen grandchildren.

TOM JENKINS, a leading innovator and entrepreneur, is chair and former CEO of OpenText, Canada's largest software company, headquartered in Waterloo, Ontario. Born in Hamilton, Ontario, Tom is the tenth chancellor of the University of Waterloo, chair of the National Research Council, and is an Officer of the Order of Canada (O.C.) for his contributions to education and innovation in Canada.

THE ILLUSTRATOR

JOSH HOLINATY was raised in Alberta and now works out of Toronto, Ontario. He has worked with a variety of clients, including the *New York Times*, *The Globe and Mail*, *Maisonneuve*, and *MoneySense*, and on a variety of illustration projects, such as editorial, ads, poster design, walls, and more. He has illustrated several children's books: *Liam Takes a Stand* by Troy Wilson, *Ira Crumb Makes a Pretty Good Friend* by Naseem Hrab, *It's Catching* by Jennifer Gardy, and *A Beginner's Guide to Immortality* by Maria Birmingham (nominated for the 2016 Norma Fleck Award).